P9-DFL-622

BEING
KADDISH

BEING KADDISH

BY

DUDLEY WEINBERG

HOUSE OF PEACE PUBLISHING

Being Kaddish
Copyright © 2019 by Myra Diaz, House of Peace Publishing
All rights reserved. No portion of this publication may be reproduced in
any form without written consent from the publisher.
Printed in the United States of America

first edition
ISBN: 978-0-578-50163-5
Published by House of Peace Publishing

cover art: Marian Weinberg
cover and author photos: Bill Davison
calligraphy: Myra Diaz
graphic design: Lawrence Didona
                    Myra Diaz

Introduction

Throughout his distinguished career Rabbi Dudley Weinberg— our dad— faithfully served his congregations and greater communities, most notably those in Boston and Milwaukee. From 1955 until his passing in 1976, he tended Milwaukee's congregation Emanu-El B'nai Jeshurun as beloved guide, teacher, and friend to many. Through his leadership and ecumenical vision he fostered interfaith dialogue and was outspokenly active in the volatile civil rights and anti-war movements of the day, equitably mingling with the famous and underprivileged alike. Renowned for his wise eloquence, his distinctively deep and resonant voice yet echoes in living memory, beyond time.

This collection offers several of the reflective meditations he would frequently compose and share, in place of the standard prayer book reading that proceeds recitation of the mourners' Kaddish. Although they express certain re-occurring themes, each meditation bespeaks a unique offering of heartfelt consolation as he sought to compassionately bridge the ineffable chasm between the living and those no longer among the living. While acknowledging the sharp reality of loss and grief, he consistently gives uplifting voice to the preciousness of life's immediacy, of memory, of the bonds of love and connection to all the living, and to the striving to comprehend and attain oneness with God.

Those of us who remember his delivery of these soliloquies can yet hear the velvety resonance of his voice, the laden pause— and then: "With these thoughts in our minds and in our hearts, we speak now the names of some of our departed dear ones, the anniversaries of whose going from this life to the life of the eternal occurred during this week..."

A *saeculum* is a measure of time— the length between an event's occurrence and the passing of the last person to remember it. At the recent sad occasion of our mother's funeral, when several of these meditations were read— a kind of homage to *both* our parents— there were some in attendance stirred not only by the moving words, but by the voice yet held in their living and loving memory. Now the numbers of those who knew him are dwindling; the memory-keepers of his voice and beneficent presence, souls he touched in this life, are passing onward. It is our hope to preserve his words for those whom he affected personally and for any who might yet find uplifting guidance and consolation within their thoughtful contemplation.

We pray that these meditations continue to bring inspiration, comfort, and solace.

Jonathan Weinberg
Myra Diaz
2018

יִתְגַּדַּל וְיִתְקַדַּשׁ שְׁמֵהּ רַבָּא. בְּעָלְמָא דִי בְרָא כִרְעוּתֵהּ,
וְיַמְלִיךְ מַלְכוּתֵהּ בְּחַיֵּיכוֹן וּבְיוֹמֵיכוֹן וּבְחַיֵּי דְכָל בֵּית יִשְׂרָאֵל,
בַּעֲגָלָא וּבִזְמַן קָרִיב, וְאִמְרוּ אָמֵן.

יְהֵא שְׁמֵהּ רַבָּא מְבָרַךְ לְעָלַם וּלְעָלְמֵי עָלְמַיָּא.

יִתְבָּרַךְ וְיִשְׁתַּבַּח וְיִתְפָּאַר וְיִתְרוֹמַם וְיִתְנַשֵּׂא וְיִתְהַדָּר
וְיִתְעַלֶּה וְיִתְהַלָּל שְׁמֵהּ דְּקֻדְשָׁא בְּרִיךְ הוּא,
לְעֵלָּא מִן כָּל בִּרְכָתָא וְשִׁירָתָא תֻּשְׁבְּחָתָא וְנֶחֱמָתָא,
דַּאֲמִירָן בְּעָלְמָא, וְאִמְרוּ אָמֵן.

יְהֵא שְׁלָמָא רַבָּא מִן שְׁמַיָּא, וְחַיִּים עָלֵינוּ וְעַל כָּל
יִשְׂרָאֵל, וְאִמְרוּ אָמֵן.

עֹשֶׂה שָׁלוֹם בִּמְרוֹמָיו, הוּא יַעֲשֶׂה שָׁלוֹם
עָלֵינוּ וְעַל כָּל יִשְׂרָאֵל, וְאִמְרוּ
אָמֵן

Yitgadal v'yitkadash sh'mei raba. B'alma di v'ra chirutei, v'yamlich malchutei, b'chayeichon uv'yomeichon uv'chayei d'chol beit Yisrael, baagala uviz'man kariv. V'im'ru: Amen.

Y'hei sh'mei raba m'varach l'alam ul'almei almaya.

Yitbarach v'yishtabach v'yitpaar v'yitromam v'yitnasei, v'yit'hadar v'yitaleh v'yit'halal sh'mei d'Kud'sha B'rich Hu, l'eila min kol birchata v'shirata, tushb'chata v'nechemata, daamiran b'alma. V'imru: Amen.

Y'hei sh'lama raba min sh'maya, v'chayim aleinu v'al kol Yisrael. V'imru: Amen. Oseh shalom bimromav, Hu yaaseh shalom aleinu, v'al kol Yisrael. V'imru: Amen.

Exalted and hallowed be God's Great Name in the world which God created, according to plan. May God's majesty be revealed in the days of our lifetime and the life of all Israel— speedily, imminently. To which we say: Amen.

Blessed be God's Great Name to all eternity.

Blessed, praised, honored, exalted, extolled, glorified, adored, and lauded be the name of the Holy Blessed One, beyond all earthly words and songs of blessing, praise, and comfort. To which we say: Amen.

May there be abundant peace from heaven, and life, for us and all Israel. To which we say: Amen. May the One who creates harmony on high, bring peace to us and to all Israel. To which we say: Amen.

BEING KADDISH

What is Kaddish? Kaddish is not merely a liturgical formula. We say in our tradition that a person *is* a Kaddish, not merely that he says a Kaddish. What is Kaddish? Kaddish is the declaration that God is supreme, that His kingdom is real, that we hold the visions of it in the center of our being. Kaddish is the proclamation that God, who is above all of our blessings and all our praises, is nevertheless at the heart of our hearts and the soul of our souls, and is the Source and the Guarantor of all that is good and just and right and beautiful and holy. Kaddish is a turning outward to the world in ultimate concern, even when our own hearts are broken inside and are praying for the peace and the welfare of Israel and mankind. Kaddish is man's determined struggle to make God King in this world, to bring the peace that reigns in His high places into the places of human habitation. And a Jew is asked not simply to say Kaddish, but to be a Kaddish.

Date Unknown

The challenge is that we may be worthy of our memories, that we make our lives a continued flowering of the lives that once blessed ours. That we make of our memories a torch that illuminates, and not a fire that consumes. That we make of the love we have known a validation of the love we would give and the love that we seek. That we make of the truth bestowed to us by those who are no more, and yet are, an incentive to the truth we will transmit to our children. That we accept the uncountable riches they give unto us, their heirs, as the real riches upon which life can be made to flourish. This is the challenge— to be worthy of our memories.

Date Unknown

Reverently and tenderly now, we turn our thoughts to beloved ones who have gone on beyond the veil that separated this life from the life eternal. We speak now the names of dear ones, the anniversaries of whose departure from this life have occurred this past week.

October 18, 1955

The flower of the field is glorious in its beauty, wondrous in its fragrance, and yet it withers and is gone. *The place thereof knoweth it no more*, but it goes only to give life, for its seed blossoms again and again. There is fragrance and the memory of fragrance, beauty and the recollection of beauty. Shall we say that that which gives life has not life? Shall we say, when the mystery of death is thrust upon us, that those whose spirits kindle ours, those whose love evokes our love, those whose passions for the truth make us to serve and search after the truth— that they themselves are beyond love and beyond truth, beyond the holiness which binds us together with all who seek after the true and the good? Let us, rather, bow before the wondrous mystery that life continues, even when we see it not and know not how. Let us never consume ourselves in despair, in hopelessness, in angry rebellion. The miracle of life is greater than the life we know.

It is with these thoughts in our hearts that we speak the names of some of our beloved departed, the anniversaries of whose passing from this life to the life eternal occurred during this week. Blessed were you in your coming into the Temple of the Lord. Be blessed as you go forth to live, to love, and to serve in the temple of humanity.

February 3, 1956

Ask not that we should not suffer. Ask not even that we should not know death. Ask only that our suffering may make us gentle and pure. Ask only that our awareness of death makes us more reverent of life. Ask not that there should be not tears; ask only that our tears be shed out of love. Ask not that there be no heartache, for a stone knows no heartache. Ask only that we continue always to aspire beyond our grasp, for this is essential of our sorrow.

If we knew no love, we would never weep. If we did not yearn for a clearer and greater vision of God and His truth, we would never know sorrow, nor would we regret either our own departure or the departure of dear ones from life.

Understand that our suffering and our sorrows, hard as they are to bear, are the evidence of our blessings. They tell us who we are, as was spoken by the great Rabbi Akiva many centuries ago, when he said, "Blessed are Israel, for they are made in the image of their Creator. Doubly blessed are they, for they know that they are so made." Our sorrows, our suffering, our tears, our longing remind us who we are. It is with these thoughts in our minds that we speak now the names of the beloved departed ones, the anniversaries of whose departure from this life to the life eternal have occurred during this week.

March 30, 1956

W hat shall we do with the grief that must afflict us all? Or, rather, what shall we allow our sorrows to do to us? Shall we let them embitter us and make us hard? Shall we allow them to force us to build ramparts between ourselves and other human beings? Shall we spend the rest of our days protecting ourselves against the hurt which comes only to those who love? It is easy to grow hard. It is easy to grow bitter. It is easy to deny life and the glory of the living. But this is not the Jewish way.

In a moment, we shall speak the words of Kaddish, and they will tell us what a Jew does when his life and his hope are assailed by sorrow. He turns not only inward to himself, to lick his own wounds, but he turns outward to God and to the world. He prays not that his own will may be imposed upon a more comfortable world, but that God's will may be brought to flower in the light of mankind. He does not pour out bitter rebelliousness against the universe and against other men; he prays for the welfare and the peace of other men. Out of his own sorrow, he learns that other people too have sorrows; and from out of the community of suffering, he distills the glory of love. This is what we should do with our sorrow.

It is with these thoughts in our hearts and in our minds that we speak now the names of some of our beloved departed, the anniversaries of whose departures from this life to the life eternal occurred during this past week.

September 21, 1956

They depart from us, those dear ones upon whom we learn to rely, upon whom we stay our own weakness, from whom we derive the strength and the inspiration to uphold us in moments of our uncertainties. It is as though they have held out their hands to us and then withdrawn them. Ought it not be so? Is it not like a parent who teaches a little child to walk? Do we not hold the hand of the child, steady his steps, and then gradually withdraw from his grasp in order that he may walk with his own strength, see his way with his own spirit, lift up his eyes unafraid of the tomorrow and the tomorrow after? So too it is with teachers and parents and beloved friends who withdraw from us, where our hands can no longer touch theirs. It is as though they say to us, "Come now, be not afraid; walk, you have strength. Look, you know where to go. Believe what we have taught you well. And in walking as we have taught you, you will not be betrayed." Let their withdrawal be a part of the education of our selves, and so our sorrow, our grief, will be but a stepping stone from upon which we shall mount to higher and nobler fulfillment.

January 11, 1957

The Psalmist says, *"Karov l'Adonoi l'chol kor-av, l'chol asher yikra-uhu b'emet. God is near unto all those who seek Him; to all who seek Him in truth, He is near."* He might have added, "even to those who do not seek." However, it is only they who seek who know that the salvation of the Lord is always at hand. His faithfulness is beyond measure. Even within the limitations of the life we know, we know His salvation. Every time the sentiments of love enter our hearts, every time we reach out a hand to another creature in concern and care, every time we lift our eyes to the broader horizons, the truth is evident: This is God's salvation, this is His faithfulness. So that when men seek Him, they shall find Him. And if, within this life, with all its inadequacies, with all its shortcomings, with all its stupidities, and all its ignorance and wickedness, we nevertheless know the fruits of God's faithfulness, how much the more must it be so beyond this life, when the limitations of time and of space are dropped, and the freedom of eternity breaks! We who trust God to save us here must surely trust Him, with confidence and joyous hope, to deliver us and our beloved ones then.

It is with these realizations in our thoughts and in our hearts that we speak now the names of some of our beloved ones.

February 1, 1957

If the recollection of our beloved departed ones inspires us to prayer, let our prayer be worthy of them. Let our prayer be not for the healing of our own hurt, but rather for the outreach of our hearts to other broken hearts. Let us remember our departed by serving the truth that they served when they were at their best. Let us establish their memory by building castles of beauty and goodness in the wilderness of our world. Let our recalling be the focusing of our lives upon objects worthy of our departed ones. So shall our remembering be as blessings, our recollections be fruitful, our tears be as the summer rain on a parched field.

With these thoughts in our minds and in our hearts, we speak now the names of some of our beloved departed ones, whose anniversaries of going from this life to the life eternal occurred this week.

March 15, 1957

Reverently and tenderly now, we think of beloved ones who live now and yet are beyond the touch of our hands and the sight of our eyes and the hearing of our ears. We speak the names of some of them, the anniversaries of whose departure from this life to the life eternal occurred during this week.

The Psalmist said that, in his affliction, he learned the law of God. Indeed, purposeful will be the grief we suffer, if it sends us back to serve and to bless the living, if we learn how to counsel and to comfort those who, like ourselves, are sorrow stricken.

Though absent, the departed still minister to our spirits, teaching us patience, faithfulness, and devotion. Within the circle of daily association, we often fail to discern their worth and their loveliness, while in the remembrance of their virtues and affections, the best and purest part of their nature lies eternally enshrined.

Let us then lift our heads in hope, and summon our strength for duty. We dwell in the shelter of the Almighty, for He is our refuge and our fortress.

Rise now, those of you who will, and speak with me words of faith and of courage and of hope.

June 21, 1957

Reverently and tenderly, we think now of beloved ones who have passed beyond the reach of our hands and the sight of our eyes and the sound of our ears. We speak the names of some of them, the anniversaries of whose departure from this life to the life eternal occurred during this week.

In our hearts, we speak the names of all our beloved departed. He who is our support in the struggles of life is also our hope in death. We have set Him before us and shall not despair. In His hands are the souls of all the living and the spirits of all flesh. Under His protection we abide, and by His love are we comforted.

O, Life of our life, Soul of our soul, cause Thy light to shine into our hearts. Fill our spirits with abiding trust in Thee.

July 12, 1957

*May the time not be distant, O Lord, when Thy name shall
be worshipped in all the earth, unbelief shall disappear, and
error be no more. Fervently we pray that the day may come when all
men shall invoke Thy name, when corruption and evil shall give way
to purity and justice and goodness, and superstition shall no longer
enslave the mind nor idolatry blind the eye, when all who dwell on
earth shall know that it is to Thee alone to whom every knee must
bend, and every tongue give homage. O, may all created in Thine
image recognize that they are brethren, so that one in spirit and one
in fellowship, they may be forever united before Thee. Then shall Thy
kingdom be established on earth, and the word of Thine ancient seer be
fulfilled: The Lord will reign forever and ever.*

What do we owe to our departed beloved ones? What
do we owe them truly? We owe them the right to be seen as
human beings with faults and imperfections against which
they struggled, even as we struggle against our own. We owe
them the right to not be judged, but to be seen as we would
wish ourselves to be judged. We owe them the joyous duty of
seeing in them and in the love with which they loved us, which
binds us still to them, the miracle of God's presence and God's
outreach. And we owe them the duty of seeking to emulate
their example, without elevating them to a platform of false
perfectionism that violates both the truth and their struggle, as
well as the needs of our own.

Let us see our parents who are gone, teachers who are
departed, friends and heroes who have moved beyond the
touch of our hands as part of the great luminous struggle of the
human spirit to overcome evil, to establish the truth, to form

and to propagate that duty. Having seen the glory of the struggle to live, we will be inspired to continue the struggle with our own strength. This will be the unfading bouquet which we can place upon their resting places.

July 17, 1957

Past and future are born of man's encounter with God. For God alone there is neither past nor future; there is eternity, in which all being is summed up in immediacy. For the living or not yet living creature which is not man, there is neither past nor future. There is only the present moment. There is no recollection, there is no memory, there are no dreams, there are no plans, there is no love, there is no aspiration. But because God has touched the soul of man, eternity and the present moment we know are the parents of yesterday and tomorrow. Therefore, we can remember. Therefore, we can aspire. Know then that our memories, even though they are fraught with the burden of sorrow, are the evidence of our blessing. Know that our dreams and our love – along with the obligations they impose upon us, and the threat that they pose, which may keep us from fulfilling that to which we are called – are also the evidence of God's blessing. We remember, we love, we labor, and we hope, because God has reached out unto us and taken us into His embrace. It is in the spirit of these thoughts that we speak now the names of beloved ones who have gone beyond touch and sight and hearing and yet remain with us to bless, to inspire, to guide.

September 6, 1957

The prophet David tells us that all flesh is grass. We wither like the flower of the field, and the place thereof is unknown, and the wind passes over it as though it had never been there. How remarkable then, that we, who are from one point of view nothing, embrace everything. All truth, every vision of goodness, all beauty is within the range of our grasp. Every creative wonder is planted within us who are destined to be nothing. Man is a miraculous contradiction: Constituted chemically and biologically, he is doomed to destruction; constituted spiritually, he comes from and belongs to eternity. Every ache in our hearts, every pure passion disappointed, requited, and unrequited, all longing is evidence of the blessing with which we are blessed and of the wonder with which we have been touched by the brush of the Divine Artist. If you mourn, your very ability to mourn is one of the traces of eternity. If you look back and say, "I was less than I should have been under the promptings of my teachers and my parents, and I shall try to be more," this, too, is the etching of the eternal.

Understand then, if you mourn, that mourning is an evidence of blessing. For only they can mourn who may pass away and are yet not gone, who may disappear and yet continue to be, to live eternally in the presence of the Eternal One.

September 13, 1957

We ask, how can it be that, having died, man may yet live? How can it be that, having departed from life, man born of woman may know immortality? This is no great wonder; more wonderful by far is that, not having lived, man should have been summoned to life. That out of stones and plants and earth and air and unfeeling things, there should have been called into being a creature who lives and loves, who aspires and dreams, who can shed a tear and laugh with joy. Far more miraculous that we should ever have been ordained to life than that, having been brought to life, we should live again. The hand of God and of His miraculous work is not only in maintaining life, but in creating it. Let us remember this when we remember our beloved ones who are not, and yet are.

October 8, 1957

We speak much of harvests these days. Often we delude ourselves into thinking that the fruit we reap is of our own planting. It is rarely so. The fields were fields that we inherited. The fertility of the soil, of the spirit, and of the heart was established by those who walked and labored and loved before we did. We reap the fruit of the planting of others, and it is good to remember to think of ourselves not too highly, but to learn to bring our tribute of thanks to those who made our own lives more secure, more meaningful, sometimes more serene. We have learned that, as we have inherited, so must we create a heritage from which others who come after us will harvest fruit. It is with this kind of backward glance and forward gaze that we think of beloved departed ones, and we speak the names of some of them, the anniversaries of whose passing occur during this week.

October 11, 1957

I saw a newborn baby. It was not much different in its understanding and grasp of life than a newborn creature of the fields and the trees and the marshes, yet I knew that the life of this child had been touched with the glory that would open its soul to the farthermost reaches of God's reality. This child would know love, would give it and would seek it. This child would hunger for the truth, even if and when it betrayed him. This child would thrill to beauty, even if it besmirched itself with ugliness. And I knew, as you know, that this child and every child was fashioned according to the dimensions not of time alone, but of eternity, was snatched out of the static universe and brought into the world of the eternally living. And I knew that though that child would die, it would live.

With this thought in our hearts, we remember beloved ones who have gone beyond the veil that separates life from life.

October 18, 1957

The Talmud teaches that among the sounds which are heard from one end of the earth to the other is the cry of a baby when it is born. It is said that we object to coming into the world, because somehow we know that great demands will be made upon us: That we will be asked to live in a world in which we must die, and yet live as though we will never die; that we will be asked to love as though forever, and yet see the objects of our love disappear from our sight, be removed from our touch, and from beyond our hearing. We shall be asked to pursue a truth that we feel to be absolute, while we succeed in grasping merely some of the outer fragments of the web of truth. We must strive to be good, because we can do not otherwise, and yet we find ourselves betrayed even by our own fondest dreams and noblest ideas. Therefore, a baby cries when it is born, and the sound of its cries are heard from one end of the world to the other. This is the tragedy of life.

It is also the glory of life. And we who are bound to time and space should likewise be knit into the fabric of eternity. This is our glory. No person could love at all if their love did not mean forever. No person could go in search of truth if their search did not mean a truth that abides. No person would risk anything for goodness and justice and mercy, or even dream of them, if they did not know deep within themselves that goodness is ordained by the very Author of being. So, if we weep when the evidence of our finiteness is upon us, let us remember that the same thing that makes us weep causes our joys. If we weep because of what is taken from us, let us remember that this very taking contains what can never be taken away. Man is of today and not of tomorrow. But he is of eternity.

December 13, 1957

We weep for those who are dead. If we understand well, we will not weep, for our faith will teach us to trust God to sustain them with His love, with His truth, and with His own faithfulness. Yet we must weep— weep for the lives we ourselves do not live, for having loved less than we could, for giving less than we can, for creating less than is in us to create. Let death remind us not of the hopelessness of loss, but of the squandering of life. Let our tears wash our hearts clean, so that our vision may include the heart of another. Let our longing cause us to reach out to another human being, and then our grief will not be in vain. Let us learn that, even in this imperfect life, we see enough of God's faithfulness to trust Him for what comes afterward; and trusting, so let us give ourselves to the fulfillment of the life God gives us now.

May 16, 1958

W e stand at the threshold of the festival of the giving of the Torah, and when we are at our best, we know that it is the Torah which is the length of our days and the true wisdom of our hearts. We know, too, that it is a heritage: that we have not made it, we have received it. That it has been transmitted through love, through courage, through devotion, through heroism of the soul. We know, too, that our present and the hope of our tomorrow are the fruits of the love borne unto us from out of the past, out of all the yesteryears. Therefore, we look to the yesteryears not only with regret, not only with longing for those who were and are not, but with thanksgiving that they should have been, and that their heritage lives within us; so that they live within us, in order that we may be bearers of light and truth and love and justice as they were, and thus continue to give them life in the yet unborn future. It is in this spirit that we speak now the names of some beloved ones, the anniversaries of whose departure from this life to the life eternal have occurred during this week.

May 23, 1958

A human being must be worthy of his memories. A human being must understand the burdens of the past, while contemplating that those who gave may indeed have given to Him; that those who loved may indeed have found in Him a responsive object of their devotion; that those who taught may have found, through Him, a willing student for their teaching. If it is pain and sorrow and suffering we remember, as we are remembering them today, then we must be worthy of those memories too, and of their challenge, and of the duty they impose upon us. So shall our memories not be vain things. So shall our recollections be more than the occasion for the expression of anger, the utterance of self-pity, the speaking forth of indignation. A human being must be worthy of his memories and wrest from them a blessing for himself and for mankind. It is in this spirit that we think of the men and women across all the generations who died for the greater glory of humankind and thus in the service of God.

May 30, 1958
(Memorial Day reflection)

Someone has said that, for the pious person, it is a privilege to die. This was not a morbid statement. It was the statement of the trust and faith that grow in the heart and that flourish in the hand of a person who has learned to see the work of God wherever he turns, wherever he looks, in whatever he himself does. It is the confidence born of the ultimate question, which asks, "How could I ever have learned to love?" It is the faith that is born of the amazement that strikes the human heart, which dares to ask, "How was I ever impelled to ask for the truth?" It is the gratitude that flowers when a man knows that he is struggling to be good even when he fails, then asks, "How did it ever occur to me or to anyone else, in a world or a universe which know nothing of goodness, to strive for it?" The pious person sees the evidence of God's love and God's faithfulness wherever he turns, even in his sorrows. Therefore, when he is summoned from this life, he goes confidently, knowing that the God whose love was manifest here, where we know so little, cannot fail to continue His abiding love, where we may know yet more. It is in the spirit of these thoughts that we recall beloved departed ones...

August 29, 1958

A year has gone, a New Year has come, but in the sight of God a thousand years are but as yesterday when it is past. Our life is but a fleeting gleam between two eternities. Yet, though generations come and go, the Word of our God stands forever. Only the dust returns to the dust. The spirit returns to God who gave it. Our dear ones have passed through the gateway to the grave, to the endless peace of life eternal. All of us must inevitably tread the same path, though we know not when the hour may come. May we so live that when this hour comes, it shall find us prepared. We look unto Thee with hope, O God, firmly believing that what Thou doest is for the best, and in this faith we recall beloved departed ones, speaking the names of some of them, the anniversaries of whose departure from this life occurred on this festival in another year.

September 14, 1958
(Rosh Hashanah)

What do our memories do to us? Do they cause us to turn selfishly inward, to nurse our wounds, to accumulate angry regrets? Do they make us bitter? What sort of turnings do our memories evoke within us? Do they perhaps cause us to turn outward, because we have learned the reality and the community of sorrow? Do they make us more sensitive to the hurts inflicted upon other hearts? Do they make us more understanding of human need? Do our memories remind us that life is brief and frail, and that therefore each hour must be used in service of worthy ends, in the illumination of other lives, in that giving of ourselves which is bowing before God? What kind of turning does memory cause within us? Let it be that, as we recall the sorrow of loss, we are made to turn outward. Let it be that, as the pain of grief is renewed within us, we are made to concern ourselves for the welfare of all humanity— for every person knows pain. Then our memories will be a cause for blessing, and in our remembering we shall bring again to life the loving, creative reality of our beloved departed ones.

September 19, 1958

We must remember that the wonder is not that men die. That is not the wonder. The wonder is that they live. The wonder is not that there comes a moment when we are no longer able to communicate with dear ones through our senses, the sight of our eyes, and the hearing of our ears. The wonder is that we are ever able to communicate at all. What is there in the universe— in the great whirling, precise, unfeeling universe— that argues for life? Nothing. Not from the great fiery stars in space, not from the tiny bits of meteoric dust, not from the rocks and the rivers is there any argument for life. Life is a gift toward which our eyes ought to be opened in awesome wonder every moment. Equally great is the miracle of communication, the miracle of understanding, the wonder that unites mind to mind and heart to heart and soul to soul, so that even if there were no more of the life we know and but the single moment of connection, we would bow in gratitude, in thanksgiving, in unutterable reverence before the Author and the Giver of that life which can only be given by Him. But the Giver is of such nature that His giving is eternal. Let us therefore, in our thanksgiving for the miracle of life, also find comfort in the alteration of life and the physical removal of dear ones. We dream, as dream we must. Let our dream not be as a curtain drawn over the sight of the eye within us, which sees and knows the wonder, the miracle, the magnificence of the gift of life.

October 17, 1958

Shall we accept joy at the hand of the Lord, and not sorrow? Do we not know that it is our sorrow that lends meaning to our joy— that if it were not possible for us to love something so greatly that we can be deprived of it, then life would be empty, meaningless, and a striving after wind? Sorrow is not easy to bear, but it carries its blessing within it, if we make it not merely the pain that is imprisoned within the selfish walls of our heart, but the pain that binds us to others, thus renewing the miracle of love that blessed us and then made us mourn.

January 9, 1959

We ought not to bear grief only as a burden. We ought to unfurl it as a miracle. Why should we grieve? Why should anything in the universe grieve? That we are able to mourn is evidence that ours is a special destiny. What else mourns? When a star is extinguished, do the other stars grieve for it? When an insect falls from its flight, do the other insects shed tears? When a stone is crushed or a flower crumbles, do other stones and other flowers cry aloud in pain? Only man is able to grieve, because his life is touched with the vision that is beyond time and is not even in space. Only a human being is blessed with the blessing of love.

So when our lives are touched by grief and our hearts cry aloud more than can be uttered in words, know that our grief is not merely evidence of our troubles. It is the proof of our blessing. It is our triumph over time and space, in which all things die, and our accession to eternity, in which life is forever.

January 23, 1959

We remember, and we weep. Would you have it otherwise? Would it be better if, after life and love have been shared, there was nothing about which to weep? Would we have it so? Would not the tragedy of loss be blank and empty and meaningless if there were nothing over which to weep? Tears and sorrow are the evidence of blessing. The ache of longing is the proof that we have known good, and the pain is relieved only when the love we recall ceases to rest as a burden upon our hearts and is lightened because we share that love with others. What we have inherited is what causes us to weep. In transmitting it to the generations which are yet to be, the burden is lifted, love completes its cycle, time merges into eternity, and life is seen as immortality.

February 6, 1959

If the tears we shed may lead to laughter, then they are tears of blessing. If in recalling the pain that sorrow and separation inflict upon us, we hold out the hand of healing to others so that their faces once again smile, then our sorrow and our tears are blessed. If our remembering causes us to measure ourselves regretfully against the standards of love that taught us to aspire greatly, but then we are so moved to aspire and to know the joy that comes of our own growth, so that we laugh, then our remembering and our tears are blessed. If weeping, because we long for the evidence of love that once gave us life, we turn outward with the concern that evokes love because it gives love, and thus we bring alive the laughter born of the miracle of human communication, then our tears are blessed. Let us remember in this spirit. Let us recall our dear ones as a challenge to bring the joy of healing, the aspiration for the truth, and the renewal of love into our lives and the lives of others, so that tears may give birth to laughter.

March 7, 1959

It is only love that can set us free of the fear of death. Only love that can set us free from the bondage of angry recollection, clearing our vision, so that what is abidingly good and everlastingly blessed may remain with us. We remember dear ones, and sometimes we are afraid to remember, because in recalling we remember both our imperfections and theirs. Love sets us free— free of the anger, free of the resentment that prevents us from being better sons of good fathers, better daughters of good mothers, better pupils of good teachers. Love. Be not afraid to love, and you will not be afraid to remember. Then memory will not be simply a burden that presses the tears out of our eyes, but a banner that lifts our sights to vision yet beyond our grasp— but so sweet that we must always move toward that. And so, love will turn back our steps to the way of life.

April 24, 1959

Reverently and tenderly now, we turn our thoughts to beloved ones who are no longer within the reach of our arms and the hearing of our ears and the sight of our eyes, but who remain with us nonetheless, to bless, to guide, and to teach. And we name some of them by name, those whose anniversaries from this life to the life eternal occurred during this week.

May 1, 1959

How shall we look to the past? In what spirit shall we recall those who make our memories? Shall it not be by looking to tomorrow? What fruit will be born by the love whose object is no longer before our eyes, if we do not give ourselves to the work of love today and tomorrow? What blessing will be born of the tears, when we think of dear ones who are beyond the touch of our hand, if we do not extend those same hands to other human beings today and tomorrow? Let us remember, with a forward glance, that the recollection of parents and teachers and friends inspires to greater gentleness and profounder consecration of right and truth and love. Let our remembering be one with our aspiring, and even our grief will then become a blessing.

May 22, 1959

Tomorrow, they say, is Memorial Day. Who remembers—and what? What do we remember? We sit here in freedom, in comfort, in prosperity, and in joy, and it is hard and painful to remember that we are here as we are because blood was shed. It is difficult for us to recall that we enjoy the blessing and the hope of freedom because there have been men and women who dared both to live and to die for it. And many there have been who have died for it because the logic of history required it. Whom do we remember? And how? There are some of us who will shed some tears, because tomorrow will require us to remember losses that are close. But the shedding of tears will do no one any good, unless they are shed with humility and in repentance and in a renewed resolve to understand that the peace and the freedom for which so many human beings died must begin in our own hearts. It is the Jewish way to confess sin collectively. This is the way we do it on Yom Kippur, and this is the way we must do it tomorrow. The blood which has been shed in the world is on the hands of every one of us, and the stain can be washed away only when each one of us, in their own life, in their own way, dedicates themself to the renewal of peace, the search for brotherhood, and the assertion for freedom. Peace does not begin with the weeping of tears over the graves of our martyred dead. It begins in the imagination of our hearts and in the works of our hands. Let us remember them and link the memories of martyred departed ones with the memories of our own dear ones, the names of some of whom we speak now.

May 29, 1959

Now we speak even our sorrows, and lift them up out of the passing moment, so that upon them may shine the assurance that God's truth prevails; that His kingdom will come and will endure, and that therefore the endeavor which is life is worthy, in spite of all its sorrows and trials. It is this faith which enables us, even in the moment of our sorrow and the recollection of our loss, to reach outward and to pray for the peace, the welfare, and the salvation of others, of our own house of Israel, and of all humankind. Thus, even in our sorrows do we sanctify the Name of God and His will.

January 15, 1962

There comes a time when we reap our last harvest here on earth. For many dear ones, that harvest has been reaped, and we weep for the gathering that is to be no more. Yet we know, when we think better of it, that they have left us with a harvest that constantly renews itself, if we will but permit it. A harvest of truth, of trust, of beauty, of holiness, and of love.

We think then of beloved departed ones with gratitude, for the gifts which they have bestowed upon us as the ultimate and final harvest of their lives, and as we think of them, we pray that we may be worthy possessors of the harvest of their sowing.

October 12, 1962

The wonder is not that we die and that our dear ones die. The wonder is that we live at all. The wonder is not that memory fades. The wonder is that the truth lays hold on us in precious moments, with a clarity that defies time and place. The wonder is not that we mourn. The wonder is that we can rejoice in the blessings of love that endures, of truth that abides, of goodness— the strength of which never fail.

November 30, 1962

When yesterday's love makes its claim upon us, when the truths we were taught by faithful parents and devoted teachers stir within us, when our hearts long for the renewal of the immediate vision of those beloved ones who have been taken beyond the sight of our eyes, it is not one moment in time beckoning to another moment that is gone. It is an eternity reaching to another eternity. Nothing that arises out of the human heart in its yearning to find perfection according to God's will is but of the moment. All is of eternity. The command, the desire, the outreach, even the partial fulfillment, all are of eternity. And though the moment in which eternity breaks through may dissolve and pass away, that which has flowered remains, because it cannot perish. The love and the truth that lay their claims upon us, and for which we yearn, are the evidence that those whom we love, and we who love, are born of and are destined for that which cannot be imprisoned within time.

December 7, 1962

In love and in gratitude to those who have gone before us, who have taught us by their example, by the power of their love, and by the challenge of their kindness to us, we now think of these beloved departed ones, and we speak the names...

December 21, 1962

Miracles occur every day. The miracles of sustenance, of growth, of dreaming, of loving, of sorrow, of loving again, of hoping, these are miracles that occur every day, and the miracle of remembering, too, is one that is always with us.

The past is dead, and the past lives. This moment is gone as we grasp it, and yet it lives in the morrow which is yet unborn.

The treasures of all the yesteryears, for which we long and over which we weep, are ours if we will but claim them and let them work in our lives for blessing on the morrow.

It is in this spirit that we must remember beloved ones who have gone from us, so that our remembering becomes not a burden but a blessing, not a task but a glory.

February 15, 1963

It is inevitable that man should mourn. We mourn because our feet are planted in the soil, and our souls reach up to heaven farther than our hands can grasp. We know more life than we can live, more truth than we can speak, more love than we can enact, more justice than we can do. And we mourn because we are embarrassed by the richness of our blessing. Let us remember it well, when we think of beloved ones who are gone, and when tears flow and the heart aches. Remember how blessed we are to be able to care, to want, to feel guilty, to be inspired, to hope. It would be easier, perhaps, if we could not mourn. But then we would not be human either, and both the tragedy and the glory would be denied us. In God's wisdom we are given both. Let us face the one and be nourished by the other.

December 6, 1963

To see everything means to see pain. To see everything is to see trouble and sorrow. To see everything is to see every human enterprise fail. Yet, to see everything is to see that people suffer most for what is most beautiful and what is most good. To see everything is to see every human enterprise fail, because people at their best reach far beyond what they can grasp. To see everything and to weep is to weep because man can be so noble. To remember everything is to remember where we failed and to know that we remember it so, because there were those who taught us to strive beyond the level of even our highest achievements. To mourn is to pay tribute to the nobility of all the yesterdays and to pledge oneself to the fulfillment of the sweetest, the grandest, and the most noble dreams in all the tomorrows.

January 10, 1964

Memory is like a jewel. It requires a setting, that its brilliance may be most beautifully shed on its surroundings. When we remember beloved ones, remember them with gratitude and blessing and kindness. Let our remembering be set in the setting of a life worthy of their memory. Let that life be made pure. Let that life be dedicated to the clearing away of the roughness and the debris that we accumulate in our souls, in our relationships, in our community. Let it be a setting fit for the love and the truth, the dreams and the hopes we remember, when we remember our dear ones. To merely remember is to achieve nothing, but to remember in the midst of life and then make life itself worthy of what we remember, that is to do almost everything.

January 17, 1964

We hope prayerfully that we may be worthy of what was best and noblest in our departed ones, that in our aspirations and in the works of our hands we may bring fulfillment to what remained unfinished in their lives, that we may bring to blossom seeds that they planted, sometimes unknowingly, and make the sweet fruit of their aspirations available to nourish lives even yet unborn.

June 19, 1964

They teach us, they strike sparks from us, they give us beauty and intimations of beauty. If we allow ourselves to draw near to them with all their imperfections, truth comes from the drawing near, and then they are taken from us, and the only tribute we can pay, truly, is that we draw near to others and confer upon them the gift of beauty achieved and yet to be achieved, of truth obtained and yet to be revealed, of love granted and ever to be renewed. For the departed themselves, we trust the good Lord, but for we who need to continue in love, the living are the means with which we speak our loyalty to the dead.

July 10, 1964

There are in our midst those upon whom sorrow has been visited, those, perhaps all of us, who recall sorrow. What shall we do with the burden of our grief? What shall we do with our sorrow? We can, if we will, let it embitter us, but we can, if we will, let it bind us more sympathetically and more tenderly to others. We can let our sorrow send us out to minister and to serve. We can let our sorrow thrust us into the inner chambers of the hearts of other human beings, feeling what makes life hard for them, lending our strength to them, lending the courage we have acquired because we have lived through dark days like them and make our sorrow into a blessing. We grieve because we have known the richness life can produce. The healing of grief confers that same richness upon other lives. Let our sorrow be translated into *mitzvot*, the deeds that sanctify and sustain and nourish life. If that be the manner of our grieving, then our departed ones will work blessing even in their distance from us, as they did in their nearness.

July 24, 1964

It is only within the context of faith that we can ever find comfort for sorrow. If this is not God's universe and neither our lives nor our deaths have any abiding meaning, and if God's purpose is not enacted in our lives and in the life of humanity and history, then neither our loving nor our hating, our remembering nor our forgetting, our grieving nor our rejoicing are of any consequence. It is only within the knowledge, within the innermost chambers of the heart, of the intuition embedded within the inmost center of our thinking, that the universe is real— that it lives and that we live in its life. There is one who is the Author of that life and of ours, so that our tears, our regrets, our joyous memories, and our hopes have reality. If now we mourn because we remember, let us mourn within the context of faith that triumphs. If we look to the yesterdays that are gone, let us likewise look within the cycle that comprises all the past and all the future yet to be, within the living presence of the God who makes us one, who in His conferring of life triumphs over our deaths.

July 31, 1964

May our memories be joyous. Surely it was not intended that the miracle of recollection, which keeps dear ones near to us even when they are beyond our reach and our side, should be a burden. Surely it is not intended that the one who transcends space and time in separation should be a blight upon our spirits. When we think of dear ones who have been summoned beyond the life we know here and now, let not our thinking inflict a paralysis upon our lives. Let it not be a weight so heavy that we are unable to move further along the path of life and love. Remember: Enjoy, else the remembering is almost a repudiation.

If indeed we weep— and weep we do— we weep because we have known the blessing of love, the wonder of concern received and given, the miracle that unites separate persons in a communion so profound that it cannot be captured in words. Remember in joy, and if we must weep, and weep we often must, let our tears be tears of gratitude. Let our tears acknowledge that our lives have been touched by beauty, by redeeming truth, by a blessing given and never taken back.

October 5, 1964

It is when we understand life as the unlikely miraculous vessel in which the commanding Word is contained, from which the pure light of human beauty and goodness and justice is struck, that even when we face what seems to us the sadness of life, the termination of life, we may rise high, as if our spirits will soar to praise the God who is the Giver of life, the Sustainer of life, and the Speaker of the Word that commands life.

January 25, 1965

What can we do for the dead that we didn't do when they were alive? Of what avail is our remembering? We can relieve the burden of our own consciences, since none of us were everything to them we might have been. No human being is everything to any human being that he might be. This is part of the problem of being human. But God, in His wisdom, did not create us perfect and left us the amazing task of creating ourselves. What can we do for the dead that we did not do for them while they were living? We can be to others all that our deceased wanted to be to us, and that they, in their own imperfection and humanity, did not succeed in being. We can be as much as they were and more— more perfect in our love, more secure in our integrity, more discerning of the needs of others, more faithful in our adherence to the life that is given us. That is what we can do for the dead which we may not have done while they were the living. That is what they always wanted of us, that is what is asked of us. That is the great gift which the Creator confers upon us. Let our remembering then be a growing, let our remembering be more being, let our remembering be for blessing.

October 1, 1965

Life and death are both unbelievable. On purely logical grounds, if one could project oneself back to a time before there was life, it would never have been possible, I think, to predict that one day there would be life. And not alone life in the sense of something that quivers and pulsates and reproduces, but life of the sort that reaches and hopes and yearns and loves and makes mistakes, and hopes and reaches and loves again. Life is utterly unbelievable.

And so, too, is death. Is it truly possible to believe that, once having been summoned into existence, the marvel that we call life should be expunged from existence? Is there a person alive who can really imagine his own death? He may think it, but he cannot make himself see it.

Life is a mystery and a wonder from beginning to end— if there is a beginning, and if there is an end. We ponder it in moments of remembering, the feelings of gratitude and awe and wonder that are beyond all expression. With such feelings, we call to mind beloved departed ones who have blessed us with their struggles and with their beauty and their mistakes.

December 27, 1974

A wise teacher taught: "A man ought so to understand his life that he thanks God for that which he experiences as evil and sorrowful, even as he thanks Him and praises Him for that which he understands to be good." It is our way to preserve a tough and durable faith in life and in its hope, and to see in every situation that life may present— even the sorrowful situation which tears us away from beloved ones— the opportunity to let life assert itself through us with greater purity, more glorious nobility, and with more genuine love. So many questions occur to us when we mourn and when we remember mourning. Most of them are rhetorical and only express our weakness, our despair, our confusion. Ultimately, there is but one question. The faithful and understanding Jew asks, "What is the next *mitzvah*?" What is the next good, right, just, loving, helpful, healing thing to do? And he glories if he understands the wonder that is given to him to do just such an act. It is with such thoughts that we call beloved departed ones to mind.

Date Unknown

In nature's ebb and flow God's eternal law abides. When tears dim our vision and grief crowds our understanding, we often lose sight of His eternal plan. Yet we know that growth and decay, life and death all reveal His presence. He who is our support in the struggles of life is also our hope in death. We have set Him before us and shall not despair. In His hands are the souls of all living and the spirits of all flesh. Under His protection, we abide. By his love, we are comforted.

Date Unknown

Dudley Weinberg was born in St. Louis in 1915, the eldest of three sons of Russian immigrant parents. Prodigiously overcoming the hardships and disadvantages of poverty, he entered Carleton College at the age of sixteen and then attended rabbinical school at Hebrew Union College in Cincinnati, graduating in 1941. During those years he met and married his wife, Marian. Although pacifist by temperament and ethos, the advent of World War II called upon him to serve Jewish servicemen in harm's way, and he attended chaplain school at Harvard University before being deployed with the armed forces in New Guinea and the Philippines. There he attained the rank of Major, receiving the Bronze Star. After the war, he became assistant rabbi at Temple Israel in Memphis, followed by a position as senior rabbi at Congregation Ohabei Shalom

in Boston from 1948 to 1955. With their three children, he
and Marian then moved to Milwaukee, where he guided
Congregation Emanu-el Bnai Jeshurun until his passing in
1976. Over the years, he was actively outspoken in the civil
rights and anti-war movements, was a founding member of
the Interfaith Conference of Greater Milwaukee, and formed
the Wisconsin Council of Rabbis. He served on the Executive
Board of the Central Conference of American Rabbis, was
a trustee of the Union of American Hebrew Congregations,
and was chairman of the CCAR-UAHC Joint Commission on
Worship, and chairman of the UHAC, HUC-JIR, and CCAR
Platform Committee. Additionally, Rabbi Weinberg was an
accomplished violinist and spirited raconteur. He was beloved
by his congregation and community, leaving an enduring legacy
as eloquent orator, compassionate counselor, and friend.

ACKNOWLEDGMENTS

Our deep appreciation and gratitude to Elaine Stark for her caring, conscientious preparation of the manuscript; to Lawrence Didona for his graphic design expertise; to Bill Davison for his photographic reproductions of the cover and author; and to Marian Weinberg for her beautiful oil painting c. 1960s. Certainly she never imagined that it would enhance the cover of a book, much less a collected volume of her husband's words.

The flowers of the field... the place thereof... PSALM 103
God is near unto those who seek Him... PSALM 145
in his affliction, he learned the law of God... PSALM 119
May the time not be distant... UNION PRAYER BOOK

Made in the
USA
Middletown, DE

73978993R00040